Fenestrae Fidei
A Coloring Companion to Catholic Mosaic

Sean Fitzpatrick

Hillside Education
475 Bidwell Hill Road
Lake Ariel, PA 18436

©2007 Hillside Education, Sean Fitzpatrick
All rights reserved.

Unless you are the original purchaser and are making copies for your own
family or classroom (in other words, for noncommercial use), it is illegal to photocopy
or reproduce this material in any form without permission.

All artwork in this coloring book was created by Sean Fitzpatrick.
Some pieces were based on traditional icons of the saints or suggested by a photograph.
Any omission of credits is unintentional. The publisher requests documentation for future
printings.
Cover image created by Sean Fitzpatrick and colored by Isabel Helena Braga-Henebry.
Cover design by Ted Schluenderfritz

Annotations by Sean Fitzpatrick.

All Scripture quotations are taken from the Douay-Rheims Bible.

List of Illustrations

January
Mary, the Mother of God*
Epiphany*
Baptism of Our Lord
Our Lady of Altagracia *

February
St. Brigid*
St. Scholastica*
St. Valentine*
Ash Wednesday

March
St. Katherine Drexel
St. Patrick*
St. Joseph*
Annunciation

April
Palm Sunday*
Easter *
Divine Mercy
St. George*

May
St. Pascal Baylon*
John Paul II   *
St. Joan of Arc
Ascension

June
St. Kevin*
St. Columcille*
St. Anthony of Padua
Pentecost*

July
St. Benedict*
St. Christopher*
Our Lady of Mount Carmel
St. Ignatius of Loyola

August
St. Clare
St. Dominic
Assumption of the Blessed Virgin
St. Augustine

September
St. Peter Claver
Blessed Mother Teresa*
St. Wenceslaus
St. Jerome*

October
St. Therese
Guardian Angels*
St. Francis of Assisi*
St. Tekla of Ethiopia*

November
All Saints Day*
St. Martin de Porres
St. Cecilia
Christ the King

December
St. Nicholas
St. Lucy
The Nativity of Our Lord*
St. Stephen

*A picture book about this saint or event is featured in *Catholic Mosaic* by Cay Gibson

If anyone asks you about your faith, take him to church and show him the icons.
—St. John Chrysostom

Mary, the Mother of God
January 1

Mary, Mother of God is the title of the Blessed Mother which was first used by Elizabeth at the visitation. "In those days Mary set out and went with haste to a Judean town in the country, where she entered the house of Zechariah and greeted Elizabeth. When Elizabeth heard Mary's greeting, the child leaped in her womb. And Elizabeth was filled with the Holy Spirit and exclaimed with a loud cry, "Blessed are you among women and blessed is the fruit of your womb. And why has this happened to me, that the mother of my Lord comes to me? For as soon as I heard your greeting, the child in my womb leaped for joy. And blessed is she who believed that there would be a fulfillment of what was spoken to her by the Lord" (Luke 1:39-45). The names of Mary and Jesus are written in Greek in the icon. Mary, Mother of God is the patron of mothers and cooks.

Epiphany
January 6

"When Jesus therefore was born in Bethlehem of Juda, in the days of King Herod, behold, there came wise men from the east to Jerusalem, saying, where is he that is born king of the Jews? For we have seen his star in the east, and are come to adore him. And behold the star which they had seen in the east, went before them, until it came and stood over where the child was. And seeing the star they rejoiced with exceeding great joy. And entering into the house, they found a child with Mary his mother, and falling down they adored him; and opening their treasures, they offered him gifts; gold, frankincense, and myrrh" (Matthew 2:1-2, 9-11).

Baptism of Our Lord

"Then cometh Jesus from Galilee to the Jordan, unto John, to be baptized by him. But John stayed him, saying: I ought to be baptized by thee, and comest thou to me? And Jesus answering, said to him: Suffer it to be so now. For so it becometh us to fulfill all justice. Then he suffered him. And Jesus being baptized, forthwith came out of the water: and low, the heavens were opened to him: and he saw the Spirit of God descending as a dove, and coming upon him. And behold a voice from heaven, saying: This is my beloved Son, in whom I am well pleased" (Matthew 3:13-17).

Our Lady of Altagracia
January 21

Our Lady of Altagracia is the patron saint of the Dominican Republic. The portrait of Mary as Our Lady of Altagracia was brought to the Dominican Republic by two Spanish brothers who were early settlers of the island. Measuring only 13 by 18 inches, it is venerated as a sacred image by the people of the Dominican Republic almost as the image Our Lady of Guadalupe is venerated in North America. The people see the Blessed Mother in this image watching tenderly over the island and spreading Christianity among them. The feast day is faithfully celebrated by all-night vigils, singing, dancing, feasting, and all manner of festivity.

St. Brigid
February 1

St. Brigid was the daughter of a Scottish pagan king and a Christian slave who had been baptized by St. Patrick. Brigid remained with her mother until she was old enough to serve her father. As a child, she could not bear to see anyone suffering cold, hunger or disease. She often gave valuable goods that belonged to her father to the poor souls that she happened across. In her father's exasperation with her, he tried to sell her to the King of Leinster. Finally, to rid himself of her, he gave Brigid her freedom. She returned to her mother, who was in charge of her master's dairy. Brigid took over the job, and caused the dairy to prosper marvelously though she gave away much of the produce. Her mother was freed because of Brigid's good work. Brigid returned to her father, who arranged a marriage for her. She ran away to Bishop Mel, a student of St. Patrick, and took her first vows. It is said that she prayed that her beauty be taken from her so that she would not be sought after as a bride. Her prayer was granted her, but her beauty returned after she took her final vows. At the request of Bishops, Brigid founded convents all over Ireland. Brigid is often depicted holding an unusual cross. According to legend, Brigid wove this form of cross out of rushes at the deathbed of her pagan father. She explained the cross to her father and brought about his conversion. She is the patron saint of dairymaids, nuns, and blacksmiths.

St. Scholastica
Febraury 10

St. Scholastica was born of nobility and was the twin sister of St. Benedict. Scholastica's entire life was devoted to seeking God. She became a nun and founded a community for women which followed the rule of St. Benedict. She maintained a close bond with her brother and was greatly influenced by him. They loved to speak together for long hours about the joys of the spiritual life. One evening when Scholastica and Benedict were conducting a spiritual conversation, Benedict announced that he must depart. Scholastica begged him to stay, but he refused. She bent her head in prayer. When she looked up, the sky erupted in a great storm. Benedict rebuked her soundly. Scholastica replied that while Benedict would not listen to her entreaties, God heard them and was pleased to grant them. They remained in conversation the remainder of the night. Three nights later, Benedict was praying in his cell. He chanced to look out the window and there he saw the soul of Scholastica ascending into heaven in the form of a dove. St. Scholastica is the patron saint of nuns, convulsive children, and against storms.

St. Valentine
February 14

Although very little is known about St. Valentine of Rome, it is thought that he was a bishop and physician. The legends of him say that he was accused of giving aid to imprisoned Christians before they were martyred. After refusing to deny Christ before the Emperor Claudius in the year 280, he was sentenced to death by the sword. Before his sentence, however, Valentine converted his jailer by restoring sight and hearing to his young daughter. The origin of St. Valentine as the patron of lovers is also obscure. Some say that it is because his feast day is celebrated in the month regarded as a special time for lovers by a pagan Roman custom. St. Valentine's name was given to the old Roman holiday by church officials to suppress any pagan traditions or practices. St. Valentine is the patron saint of love, engaged couples, happy marriages, and epilepsy.

Ash Wednesday

Temptation of Jesus in the Desert

"Then Jesus was led by the spirit into the desert, to be tempted by the devil. And when he had fasted forty days and forty nights, afterwards he was hungry. And the tempter coming said to him: If thou be the son of God, command that these stones be made bread. Who answered and said: It is written, *Not in bread alone doth man live, but in every word that proceedeth from the mouth of God.* Then the devil took him up into the holy city, and set him upon the pinnacle of the temple, and said to him: If thou be the Son of God, cast thyself down, for it is written: *That he hath given his angels charge over thee, and in their hands shall they bear thee up, lest perhaps thou dash thy foot against a stone.* Jesus said to him: It is written again: *Thou shalt not tempt the Lord thy God.* Again the devil took him up into a very high mountain, and shewed all the kingdoms of the world, and the glory of them, and said to him: All these will I give thee, if falling down thou wilt adore me. Then Jesus saith to him: Begone, Satan: for it is written, *The Lord thy God shalt thou adore, and him only shalt thou serve.* Then the devil left him; and behold angels came and ministered to him." (Matthew 4:1-11)

St. Katherine Drexel
March 3

St. Katharine Drexel was born into a very wealthy family. Though Katharine was surrounded by every comfort as a child, she was unspoiled by money and was taught at an early age to use it to aid those less fortunate. After spending three years nursing her mother through a fatal illness, Katharine struck out on her own. She had a tender concern for the well being of the poor Native Americans and African Americans. She was very interested in the work of the Native American missions. She donated not only much of her time, but millions of the family fortune to these missions. St. Katharine entered the novitiate of the Sisters of Mercy, and later founded her own order: the Sisters of the Blessed Sacrament for Indians and Colored in Santa Fe, New Mexico. This order thrives today, but is simply known as the Sisters of the Blessed Sacrament. St. Katharine spent much time in travel establishing Catholic schools for African and Native Americans and founding mission centers throughout the United States. She also started the first university solely for African Americans in New Orleans. St. Katharine was compelled to stop her active life of travel and mission work when her health failed. Her last twenty years were spent in prayer and meditation.

St. Patrick
March 17

At the age of sixteen, St. Patrick was kidnapped from England by Irish raiders. He was then taken to Ireland, where he was sold as a slave to an Irish chieftain. There he tended his master's flocks as a shepherd. While watching the sheep, Patrick prayed and grew in his faith. After six years of servitude, Patrick had a dream in which he was instructed to flee Ireland and return to England. He escaped and proceeded to study in several European monasteries. He was ordained a priest, and later became a bishop. He remained in Britain for awhile and evangelized there, but his thoughts turned toward Ireland. At the behest of Pope Saint Celestine I, Patrick was sent to Ireland with the mission of converting the Irish race. He founded churches and instructed the people with great energy and enthusiasm. Several times he was taken prisoner and sentenced to death. Each time, God rescued him so that his mission might be completed. Over a period of thirty-three years, Patrick successfully converted Ireland. His ministry there has had an effect that has carried over to the present day, earning him the title of Apostle of Ireland. St. Patrick is the patron saint of Ireland and against snakes.

St. Joseph, Spouse of Mary
March 19

"Now the generation of Christ was in this wise. When as his mother Mary was espoused to Joseph, before they came together, she was found with child of the Holy Ghost. Whereupon Joseph her husband, being a just man, and not willing publicly to expose her, was minded to put her away privately. But while he thought on these things, behold the angel of the Lord appeared to him in his sleep, saying: Joseph, son of David, fear not to take unto thee Mary thy wife, for that which is conceived in her, is of the Holy Ghost. And she shall bring forth a son: and thou shalt call his name JESUS. For he shall save his people from their sins. And Joseph rising up from sleep, did as the angel of the Lord had commanded him, and took unto him his wife. And he knew her not till she brought forth her first born son: and he called his name JESUS" (Matthew 1:18-21, 24-25).

Annunciation
March 25

"And in the sixth month, the angel Gabriel was sent from God into a city of Galilee, called Nazareth, to a virgin espoused to a man whose name was Joseph, of the house of David; and the virgin's name was Mary. And the angel being come in, said unto her: Hail, full of grace, the Lord is with thee: blessed art thou among women. Who having heard, was troubled at his saying, and thought with herself what manner of salutation this should be. And the angel said to her: Fear not, Mary, for thou hast found grace with God. Behold thou shalt conceive in they womb, and shalt bring forth a son; and thou shalt call his name Jesus. He shall be great, and shall be called the Son of the most High; and the Lord God shall give unto him the throne of David his father; and he shall reign in the house of Jacob forever. And of his kingdom there shall be no end. And Mary said to the angel: How shall this be done, because I know not man? And the angel answering, said to her: The Holy Ghost shall come upon thee, and the power of the most High shall overshadow thee. And therefore also the Holy which shall be born of thee shall be called the Son of God. And behold thy cousin Elizabeth, she also hath conceived a son in her old age; and this is the sixth month with her that is called barren: Because no word shall be impossible with God. And Mary said: Behold the handmaid of the Lord; be it done to me according to thy word. And the angel departed from her" (Luke 1:26-38).

Palm Sunday

"And when they were drawing near to Jerusalem and to Bethania at the mount of Olives, he sendeth two of his disciples, and saith to them: Go into the village that is over against you, and immediately at your coming in thither, you shall find a colt tied, upon which no man yet hath sat: loose him, and bring him. And if any man shall say to you, What are you doing? Say ye that the Lord hath need of him: and immediately he will let him come hither. And going their way, they found the colt tied before the gate without, in the meeting of two ways: and they loose him. And some of them that stood there said to them: What do you loosing the colt? Who said to them as Jesus had commanded them; and they let him go with them. And they brought the colt to Jesus; and they lay their garments on him, and he sat upon him. And many spread their garments in the way: and other cut down boughs from the trees, and strewed them in the way. And they that went before and they that followed, cried, saying: Hosanna, blessed he that cometh in the name of the Lord. Blessed be the kingdom of our father David that cometh: Hosanna in the highest" (Mark 11:1-10).

Easter

"And they departing, made the sepulcher sure, sealing the stone, and setting guards. And in the end of the sabbath, when it began to dawn towards the first day of the week, came Mary Magdalen, and the other Mary, to see the sepulcher. And behold there was a great earthquake. For an angel of the Lord descended from heaven, and coming, rolled back the stone and sat upon it. And his countenance was as lightning, and his raiment was as snow. And for fear of him, the guards were struck with terror and became as dead men. And the angel answering, said to the women: Fear not you; for I know that you seek Jesus who was crucified. He is not here, for he is risen, as he said. Come, and see the place where the Lord was laid. And going quickly, tell ye his disciples that he is risen: and behold he will go before you into Galilee; there you shall see him. Lo, I have foretold it to you. And they went out quickly from the sepulcher with fear and great joy, running to tell his disciples. And behold Jesus met them, saying: All hail. But they came up and took hold of his feet, and adored him. Then Jesus said to them: Fear not" (Matthew 27:66, 28:1-10).

Divine Mercy
First Sunday after Easter

In the 1930's, St. Faustina was visited by Jesus in a vision. He gave Faustina the duty of spreading a message of His mercy to the world. He wanted her to inform the world that His mercy extends to each individual person as well as to the human race as a whole. Jesus told Faustina to paint His image as He appeared to her, and under the image He requested that the following words be inscribed: "Jesus, I trust in you." This painting is now venerated throughout the world. In these visitations, Jesus asked on numerous occasions that a feast be held in honor of His Divine Mercy on the first Sunday following Easter. On the occasion of the canonization of Sister Faustina, Pope John Paul II had the Feast of Divine Mercy officially established.

St. George
April 23

The story most commonly associated with St. George is known as the Golden Legend. As this legend would have it, in a great lake in Libya lived a fearsome dragon. This creature was so powerful that several armies were defeated by it. The dragon ate two sheep daily. When sheep were scarce, a maid from the village was chosen to be given as food instead. St. George entered the country and heard the story of the dragon on the same day that a princess was to be offered as food. St. George crossed himself and engaged in a battle against the beast. With one strike of his lance, the dragon was slain. He was rewarded by the king, but gave all that he earned to the poor. Because of this legend, St. George is most often pictured slaying a dragon or a demon. He was, however, a Roman soldier who was martyred after professing his faith. St. George is the patron saint of England, chivalry, and boy scouts.

St. Pascal Baylon
May 17

Pascal was the son of very pious peasants. At an early age, Pascal showed an uncommon devotion to the Holy Eucharist. His great love for the Holy Eucharist and for the Blessed Mother form the two most prominent characteristics of his nature. From the age of seven until the age of twenty-four, Pascal served as a shepherd. While he tended the sheep, Pascal passed the time devoutly whispering prayers. Though Pascal never received a formal education, he taught himself to read and write. He composed many beautiful prayers and meditations. St. Pascal joined the Franciscan brothers as a lay brother and spent his life in continual prayer and contemplation. He was well known for his humility and outstanding works of charity to the poor and afflicted. St. Pascal's charity was considered extraordinary even by the high standards of the Franciscans. While traveling in France, Pascal defended the dogma of the Real Presence against the blasphemies of a Calvinist preacher. In consequence, Pascal had to flee from a dangerous mob of angry Huguenots who sought to kill him. He was well respected by both rich and poor alike; both sought his counsel and friendship. St. Pascal Baylon is the patron saint of cooks and Eucharistic congresses and organizations.

John Paul II
May 18, 1920 – April 2, 2005

Born in Wadowice, Poland, young Karol Wojtyla felt called to the priesthood. After two accidents which nearly cost him his life during the German occupation of Poland, Karol secretly completed his seminary studies and was ordained a priest on May 1st, 1946. Devoted to the teachings of St. Louis de Montfort and St. John of the Cross, he earned his doctorate in theology from Rome in 1948. After years of serving as parish priest and professor in the diocese of Krakow, he was chosen as Auxiliary Bishop of Krakow in 1958 by Pope Pius XII, and later in 1963, Archbishop by Pope Paul VI. After serving prominently in the second Vatican Council, Paul VI appointed Archbishop Wojtyla a Cardinal in 1967. On the 16th of October, 1978, he ascended to the throne of Peter as John Paul II, becoming the first non-Italian pope in over 450 years. Pope John Paul II became the most traveled pope in history, visiting nearly every country in the world, and as the Vicar of Christ consecrated each country he visited to Mary. His pontificate is well-known for its strong opposition against communism, war, materialism, abortion, and other evils he called part of the "culture of death." Pope John Paul II wrote many great encyclicals, led a famous catechesis on the role of Mary as the Corredemptrix, canonized many holy men and women to the rank of saint, and was known as the pope of the youth. In 1992 he was diagnosed with Parkinson's disease and died on April 2, 2005, in Rome. On May 9th, 2005, his successor and friend, Pope Benedict XVI opened his cause for beatification.

St. Joan of Arc
May 30

At the time of Joan's life, England controlled most of France. At the age of seventeen, the voice of God came to her in a vision of St. Michael the Archangel and told her to drive the enemies of France from the land. She went to the king and told him of her divine mission. She asked to be provided with an army. The king, believing that Joan was sent by God to deliver France, awarded her an army. Joan marched into battle carrying a banner that read: "Jesus, Mary." She led her troops into victory after victory and restored the rightful king of France to his throne. Finally, she was captured by the British army and imprisoned for many months. She was put to trial and then burned to death in the marketplace as a heretic. She is the patron saint of France, captives, and martyrs.

Ascension
40 days after Easter

"They therefore who were come together, asked him, saying: Lord, wilt thou at this time restore again the kingdom to Israel? But he said to them: It is not for you to know the times or moments, which the Father hath put in his own power: But you shall receive the power of the Holy Ghost coming upon you, and you shall be witnesses unto me in Jerusalem, and in all Judea, and Samaria, and even to the uttermost part of the earth. And when he had said these things, while they looked on, he was raised up: and a cloud received him out of their sight. And while they were beholding him going up to heaven, behold two men stood by them in white garments. Who also said: Ye men of Galilee, why stand you looking up to heaven? This Jesus who is taken up from you into heaven, shall so come, as you have seen him going into heaven" (Acts 1:6-11).

Pentecost
50 Days after Easter

"And when the days of the Pentecost were accomplished, they were all together in one place: And suddenly there came a sound from heaven, as of a mighty wind coming, and it filled the whole house where they were sitting. And there appeared to them parted tongues as it were of fire, and it sat upon every one of them: And they were all filled with the Holy Ghost, and they began to speak with divers tongues, according as the Holy Ghost gave them to speak. Now there were dwelling at Jerusalem, Jews, devout men, out of every nation under heaven. And when this was noised abroad, the multitude came together, and were confounded in mind, because that every man heard them speak in his own tongue. And they were all amazed, and wondered, saying: Behold, are not all these, that speak, Galileans? And how have we heard, every man our own tongue wherein we were born?" (Acts 2:1-8)

St. Kevin
June 3

Kevin was the son of Irish nobility. He was ordained to the priesthood, and shortly thereafter retreated into a cave where he lived as a hermit for seven years. Here he spent his time in solitude and prayer. His holiness attracted many followers. This forced Kevin out of his hermitage and he founded the monastery at Glendalough, from which several other monasteries branched off. Once his monastery was well established, Kevin returned to the life of solitude that he so longed to live. While St. Kevin was not comfortable in the company of other men, he was quite at home in the company of animals. Several legends about St. Kevin depict his unusual kinship with animals. It is said that St. Kevin was in need of milk in order to feed the infant son of King Colman—the king had entrusted St. Kevin with raising him. Kevin prayed for help, and a doe arrived to feed the babe. A wolf later killed the doe. After being rebuked by St. Kevin, the wolf began to produce milk for the child herself. At another time, Kevin was praying with his arms outstretched during Lent. A blackbird came and laid an egg upon his hand. St. Kevin remained with his arms outstretched until the egg hatched. St. Kevin is the patron saint of the Archdiocese of Dublin, Ireland, and blackbirds.

St. Columcille (Columba)
June 9

St. Columcille was the son of Irish royalty. As soon as he was old enough, he left home to study for the priesthood. At his baptism he was given the name Criomhthann, but he spent so many hours in adoration of the Blessed Sacrament that his friends began to call him Columcille, which means "dove of the church." He studied under St. Finian, who strongly urged the need for missionaries in the church. Columcille befriended several who would later become great missionaries. Columcille was ordained a priest and traveled for the next seventeen years throughout Ireland. He preached, converted souls, and established over thirty churches and monasteries. He was a great scribe and taught his monks the art. These monks later created the Book of Kells. Columcille left Ireland with twelve of his disciples and founded a monastery on the island of Iona. The monastery attracted many people who were inspired by the lives of these simple monks. St. Columcille and his monks traveled among the Scottish islands preaching, converting souls and building churches. Thus Columcille gained the title of Apostle of Scotland. He remained at Iona until his death. St. Columcille is the patron saint of Scotland, bookbinders, and against floods.

(This drawing is based on an icon designed by the late Archimandrite David of Walsingham.)

St. Anthony of Padua
June 13

Anthony was ordained into the Augustinian rite, and lived in an Augustinian Abbey in Portugal. While there, he came into contact with some Franciscans who were on their way to Morocco to preach to the Muslims. He was greatly attracted to their simple way of living. He joined the Franciscan order and set off for Morocco where he hoped to die preaching the Gospel. On his journey, he was shipwrecked in Sicily. He joined some other Franciscans on their way to Assisi, and there he lived happily in utter simplicity. The simple life that he so longed to live was interrupted when he was asked to preach at an ordination when the scheduled speaker failed to arrive. He so astounded his audience with his eloquence that he was obliged to abandon his simple life. He traveled throughout Italy and parts of France evangelizing, preaching the Gospel, and teaching theology. He gained for himself the reputation of a great preacher. The infant Jesus came to Anthony in his cell. Anthony held the child in his arms in an embrace and communicated with him. Thus he is usually pictured holding the infant Jesus. St. Anthony is the patron saint of seekers of lost items, expectant mothers, and against shipwrecks.

St. Benedict
July 11

St. Benedict was of a family of Roman nobility. He was a student in Rome, but abandoned his school in dismay at the laziness and undisciplined attitude of his fellow classmates. He retreated to the mountains where he lived in a cave as a hermit for three years. During these years, food was brought to him by a raven. Inspired by his virtue, a neighborhood monastery requested him to lead them. Despite his reservations, Benedict agreed. The experiment failed; a group of monks—daunted by his extreme discipline—tried to poison St. Benedict. Eventually, he returned to his hermitage in the mountains. Though he remained a hermit, he established twelve monasteries, all guided by the Benedictine Rule. The summation of this rule is "ora et labora,"—pray and work. St. Benedict was blessed with the ability to read consciences, give prophesy, and prevent attacks of the devil. He is the patron saint of monks, spelunkers, and against poison.

Our Lady of Mount Carmel
July 16

Our Lady appeared to St. Simon Stock in 1251 in answer to his prayers for the Carmelite order. In her hand, she carried a scapular. She offered it to him, saying, "Take, beloved son, this scapular of thy order as a badge of my confraternity and for thee and all Carmelites a special sign of grace; whoever dies in this garment will not suffer everlasting fire. It is the sign of salvation, a safeguard in dangers, a pledge of peace and of the covenant." The scapular is worn by Carmelites and non-Carmelites alike; those wearing it receive the special protection of the Virgin Mother and the promise of salvation. Our Lady of Mt. Carmel is the patron saint of Carmelite Orders and the scapular.

St. Christopher
July 25

St. Christopher's fame is derived from the legend of him being a "Christ-Bearer." He was a very strong man, and lived his life wandering the world in search of adventure. In his wanderings, he came upon a hermit who lived on the edge of a dangerous stream. The hermit made his living by guiding passersby to safe places to cross the stream. He educated Christopher in the truths of our Lord. Christopher took over the hermit's job, but instead of leading the travelers to safe places to cross, he carried them across the stream himself. One day he carried a little child across the stream. The weight of this small child was so great that Christopher could barely carry him. Upon reaching the shore, the child revealed himself to be Jesus. The child was so heavy because he carried the weight of the world upon his small shoulders. Jesus then baptized Christopher in the waters of the stream. St. Christopher is the patron of travelers, traveling, and boatmen.

St. Ignatius of Loyola
July 31

St. Ignatius was born of Spanish nobility and was sent at a young age to work as a page in the royal court. He later joined the military. Ignatius received a canon ball wound to the leg while engaged in battle. This wound forced him to lie many months in bed with nothing to do but read about the lives of Christ and the saints. This time of contemplation brought about a spiritual conversion in Ignatius. He resigned his soldierly life and took a vow of poverty and chastity. He and six followers—including St. Francis Xavier—formed the Society of Jesus. Members of the Society of Jesus are known today as Jesuits. The Society of Jesus intended to go to the Holy Land to convert the Muslims, but the Turkish wars prevented them. They were sent to Rome and were ordained to the priesthood. The pope officially recognized their order and set them to work in Italy. Ignatius remained the leader of the order until his death. The constitution of the Society of Jesus that Ignatius wrote is the guide that still governs the Jesuits today. St. Ignatius of Loyola is the patron saint of Spain, the Jesuit order, and retreats.

St. Dominic
August 8

Saint Dominic was the son of Spanish nobility. He studied theology and philosophy at the University of Palencia. He was then ordained priest and later became Canon at the Cathedral of Osma. He traveled in France with his bishop and there strove to combat heresy. Dominic began to grow disheartened, for despite his efforts, heresy continued to spread. It was then that he had a vision of the Blessed Mother. She showed him a wreath of roses which represented the rosary. Mary told him that if he prayed the rosary and taught others to pray it as well, the true faith would eventually win out and conquer heresy. He founded the Order of the Friars Preachers, who are known today simply as Dominicans. This order follows the rule of St. Augustine. Many miracles are attributed to St. Dominic, including raising four people from the dead. St. Dominic is the patron saint of astronomers, the Dominican Republic, and scientists.

St. Clare
August 11

St. Clare was the daughter of a wealthy count. She was expected to marry a wealthy suitor, but at the tender age of 15 she refused him. Upon hearing St. Francis of Assisi preaching in the streets, she approached him and confided in him her longing to live for God. When she was 18, she left her home and went to the church of Our Lady of the Angels. Here she took the veil of religious profession from St. Francis. She later founded the Order of the Poor Clares, and was eventually joined by her mother and sisters. When her convent was about to be attacked by enemies of the church, Clare walked out to the convent gates carrying the Blessed Sacrament in a monstrance. She displayed it in front of the gates and prayed before it. Upon witnessing this act, the enemies fled. St. Clare is the patron saint of eyes, good weather, laundry workers, and needle workers.

Assumption
August 15

"And a great sign appeared in heaven: A woman clothed with the sun and the moon under her feet, and on her head a crown of twelve stars: and she brought forth a man child, who was to rule all nations with an iron rod: and her son was taken up to God, and to His throne" (Apocalypse 12:1, 5). On this day we celebrate Our Lady's being assumed into heaven, body and soul, where she is crowned queen of heaven and earth.

St. Augustine
August 28

St. Augustine was son to a pagan father and Catholic mother. He was brought up in the Catholic faith and taught by his mother, St. Monica. He fell away and lived a very sinful life of wild pursuits from the age of fifteen and until he was thirty. He was a great scholar, and dallied with various philosophies. Eventually, St. Augustine was converted by the unceasing and patient prayers of his mother. Augustine formed a monastery for himself and a group of friends. He was ordained to the priesthood, became a great preacher, and later became a bishop. He devoted much of his time to writings which combated the widely accepted heretical philosophies of the time. These writings earned him the honor of being a doctor of the church and are studied throughout the world today. St. Augustine is the patron saint of theologians, brewers, and printers.

Blessed Mother Teresa
September 5

Mother Teresa was the daughter of an Albanian businessman. She left home at the age of eighteen and joined the Loreto convent. A year later, the convent sent her to Calcutta, India where she taught at St. Mary's Bengali Medium School. On October 7th in the year 1950, Mother Teresa founded the Missionaries of Charity in Calcutta. The goal of this institution was to, in the words of Mother Teresa, "quench the infinite thirst of Jesus on the cross for love and souls" by "laboring at the salvation and sanctification of the poorest of the poor." She nursed the poor and diseased with a most tender and motherly love. Her devotion to the poor has inspired the world and earned her the respect and love of Christians and non-Christians alike. The Missionaries of Charity began as a simple institution in Calcutta, but has expanded not only throughout India but throughout the globe. In 1971 Mother Teresa was awarded the Pope John XXIII peace prize, and was awarded the Nobel Peace Prize in 1979. Today, the Missionaries of Charity labor in 30 countries.

St. Peter Claver
September 9

St. Peter Claver was the son of a Spanish farmer. At the age of twenty, he entered the Jesuit novitiate and was ordained a Jesuit priest. Under the encouragement of St. Alphonsus Rodriguez, Peter decided to become a missionary in America. He landed in Cartagena, Colombia. There he remained for forty-four years, evangelizing the black men and women who arrived in Cartagena to be sold as slaves. Peter was faithfully present at every ship landing. He greeted the slaves and offered them food and comforted them with his fatherly presence. Peter promised that he would remain their devoted friend and protector. It is reported that St. Peter Claver baptized and instructed in the faith more than 300,000 slaves. Aside from his work as an evangelist, Peter strove to promote humane treatment of and better conditions for the slaves on the plantations. St. Peter Claver is the patron saint of African missions, race relations, and slavery.

St. Wenceslaus
September 28

St. Wenceslaus was the son of a Bohemian duke. His father was a Christian and his mother was a pagan. Wenceslaus was instructed in the Catholic faith by his grandmother, St. Ludmilla and under her instruction, he became a Christian. When his father died, Wenceslaus became the Duke of Bohemia and took over rule of the government. He ruled Bohemia mercifully and with great charity; he conducted all his actions according to the law of God. According to an old Slavic legend about Wenceslaus, "he was charitable to the poor, and he would clothe the naked, feed the hungry, and offer hospitality to travelers according to the summons of the Gospel." When Wenceslaus had a son, his brother Boleslaus was no longer heir to the throne, and in his anger, Boleslaus murdered Wenceslaus. He later repented of his deed, and had the remains of St. Wenceslaus removed to the church of St. Vitus in Prague. Many miracles were performed at his tomb. St. Wenceslaus is the patron saint of brewers, Bohemia, and the Czech Republic.

St. Jerome
September 30

St. Jerome was born into a pagan family, and consequently led a frivolous youth. He had a lukewarm conversion in his early adulthood, but later had a true conversion while conducting theological studies. Jerome was ordained to the priesthood. He lived for several years as a hermit in the desert. According to legend, while Jerome lived in the desert he removed a thorn from a lion's paw. The lion remained by his side in faithful servitude for several years. Jerome then became secretary to Pope Damasus who requested that he translate the Bible into Latin. This work took Jerome 30 years and is known as the Vulgate translation. It is still commonly used today. He left Rome to continue his life of solitude in the desert. Here he spent much of his time in contemplation of death as well as in translating various works. Jerome is known as a doctor of the church and a father of the church. St. Jerome is the patron saint of Bible scholars, librarians, students, and translators.

St. Therese
October 1

St. Therese was born to very pious and holy parents. They nurtured and helped to develop every virtue in their children and have both been declared venerable by the church. Therese, from her earliest youth, showed signs of superior holiness. At a very young age, Therese became very ill. It was supposed by all that the illness would take her life. One day, as she was praying to the blessed mother, the statue of Mary that she was looking upon smiled at her. She was immediately cured of her illness. At the age of 15 Therese entered the Carmelite convent. There she wrote her autobiography entitled *Story of a Soul*. Therese called her path to God "the little way." By devoting herself to God's will in the most menial and simple tasks of daily life, she brought herself more closely to God. She believed in attaining perfection through humble and sincere devotion to the smallest duties. She spent only eleven years in the convent before she died of tuberculosis. St. Therese is the patron saint of African missions, ill people, and flower growers.

Guardian Angels
October 2

"See that you not despise one of these little ones: for I say to you, that their angels in heaven always see the face of my Father who is in heaven."
(Matthew, 18:10)

It is a commonly held belief that every soul has an angel appointed to guard and protect it through life, a shepherd which will help to ultimately bring the soul to God. The existence of guardian angels is supported throughout scripture. A few examples of angels in scripture include an angel of the Lord who appeared to Moses in the burning bush; the angels who appeared to Lot and saved him and his family from the burning city of Sodom; the angel Raphael who appeared to Tobit and helped him to cure his father's blindness; the angel Gabriel, who brought the message of Christ's birth to Mary; and the angel who appeared to Joseph and instructed him to flee to Egypt with his wife and child. The feast of the guardian angels was instituted that we may be reminded to venerate our faithful protectors.

St. Francis of Assisi
October 4

St. Francis was the son of a wealthy Italian merchant. He was given a good education, but led something of a wild youth. While still young, he was captured in a conflict between Assisi and Perugia and was kept as a prisoner of war. While he was held captive, he heard the voice of God calling him to abandon his worldly life. Upon his release, Francis lived according to the teachings of the Gospels. He shed his life of wealth and luxury and took on a very simple life of poverty, preaching purity and peace. Francis lived with the animals, cared for the sick—especially lepers—, preached in the streets, cleaned churches and sent food to thieves. He attracted a large following and finally founded the Franciscan order. The rule of the Franciscan order was established according to the words of Jesus: "Leave all and follow me." Francis was so closely united with Christ that he received the stigmata. St. Francis is the patron saint of animals, the Franciscan order, and merchants.

St. Tekla of Ethiopia
October 27

St. Tekla was of very humble birth, the son of Ethiopian farmers. At a very young age, Tekla fell from a tree and was crippled. Tekla desired with his whole heart to become a priest but he feared his physical defect would prevent it. In one of the many stories told about him, Tekla comes upon a wounded lion as he travels to join the monastery. Though terrified, Tekla suppresses his fear and nurses the great animal and bandages his paw. Years later, after becoming a priest, he is met on the road by the very same lion. Tekla is afraid for his life, but the lion wishes to repay Tekla's kindness, and carries him on his back to make the journey easier for the crippled saint. They set off together through the desert and convert the pagans of Ethiopia. St. Tekla was in fact a patriarch of the Ethiopian Orthodox Church and is known as the "saint who prayed on one leg" since his injured leg had withered away.

Feast of All Saints
November 1

This feast is celebrated in honor of all saints, both known and unknown. The first All Saints' Day took place on May 13th in the year 609. On that day, Pope Boniface IV received the Pantheon—an ancient Roman temple of the gods—as a gift from the Emperor Phocas. On receiving the gift, the Pope consecrated the Pantheon to the Blessed Mother and all martyrs. The pope then ordered that an anniversary of that day be kept in honor of Mary and all the martyrs. During the reign of Pope Gregory III one hundred-twenty years later, the feast day was changed to November 1st and was expanded to include all the saints. A chapel dedicated to all saints was then erected in St. Peter's church. The day was finally and officially established in the year 831 under the papacy of Gregory IV.

St. Martin de Porres
November 3

St. Martin de Porres was born in Lima, Peru, the illegitimate son of a wealthy nobleman. At an early age he studied with a renowned surgeon-barber where he had his first instruction in the art of healing and medicine. He joined the Holy Rosary Dominican Priory as a servant at the age of eleven, and was put in charge of earning funds for the order. Weekly, he earned up to two thousand dollars from the wealthy citizens of Lima. This money was used to aid the impoverished and sick of Lima. He was later put in charge of the infirmary. He had a patient devotion to the sick and was well known for his wonderful cures. Finally, the order dropped its rule forbidding black people from receiving the habit. Consequently, St. Martin took vows as a Dominican brother. He continued his work for the sick by opening a children's hospital for the poor, founding an orphanage, and establishing a home for stray dogs and cats. He found time to nurse these animals with the same care he showed his human patients. Many miraculous cures are attributed to St. Martin, including raising from the dead. St. Martin de Porres is the patron saint of barbers, public health, and inn keepers.

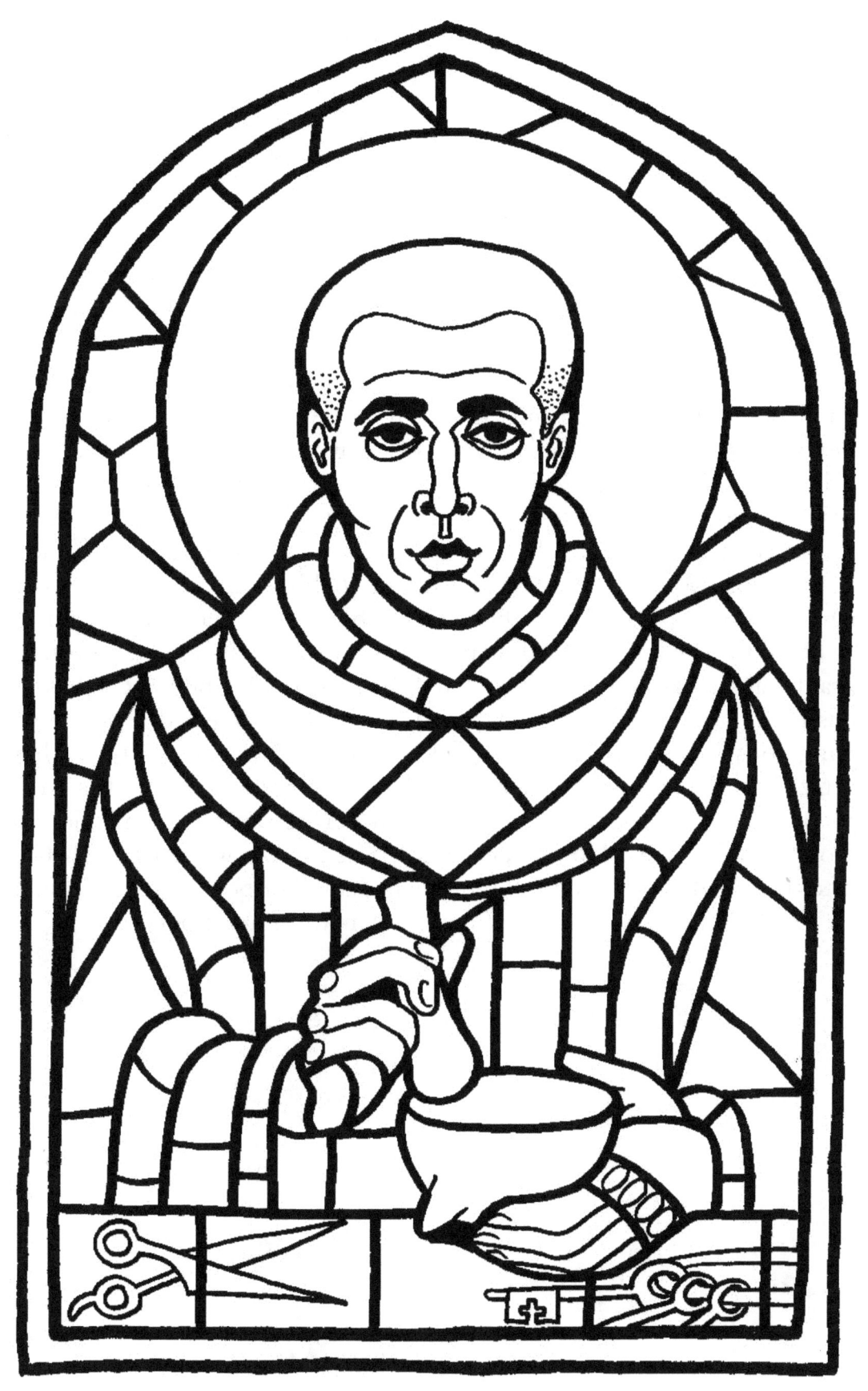

St. Cecilia
November 22

At a young age, Cecilia promised God that she would remain a virgin. Despite her wishes, her parents had her married to a pagan man by the name of Valerian of Trastevere. Cecilia sang in her heart a hymn of praise and love for Jesus while the sacrilegious, pagan music resounded at her wedding. She informed her husband that an angel always escorted her. Only upon purification would this angel be present to his sight as well. Valerian then agreed to be baptized. After the baptism, he saw Cecilia praying with an angel at her side. The angel placed a crown upon both their heads and promised to grant Valerian a favor. Valerian asked that his brother be baptized as well; his wish was granted him. Valerian and his brother engaged frequently in the dangerous practice of giving proper burial to Christian martyrs. They were arrested and martyred for their faith. Cecilia retrieved their bodies and buried them at her home. She was arrested and her persecutors demanded that she worship false gods. Upon her refusal, Cecilia too was martyred. Centuries after her death, Cecilia's tomb was opened and her body was found incorrupt. St. Cecilia is the patron saint of musicians, martyrs and poets.

Christ the King

Pilate said to Jesus, "Are you the King of the Jews?"... Jesus answered, "My kingdom does not belong to this world. If my kingdom did belong to this world, my attendants would be fighting to keep me from being handed over to the Jews. But as it is, my kingdom is not here." So Pilate said to him, "Then you are a king?" Jesus answered, "You say I am a king. For this I was born and for this I came into the world, to testify to the truth (John 18:33b, 36-37). In the year 1925, the feast of Christ the King was instituted by Pope Pius XI in his encyclical *Quas Primas*. Pope Pius XI felt that the world was embracing secularism, communism, and a wealth of other evils because of its refusal to accept Christ as sovereign over all. On the last Sunday of the Liturgical Year, we celebrate the feast of Christ the King and venerate him as ruler of the world. On this day, the world is renewed in its consecration to the Sacred Heart of Jesus.

St. Nicholas
December 6

There are many great stories associated with St. Nicholas. He was well known as being very generous to the poor and a kind protector to the innocent and mistreated. St. Nicholas once found three little boys who had been murdered and pickled in a barrel of brine. When he discovered these boys, he raised them from the dead. Stories such as this one led him to be noted as the patron saint of children. On a sea voyage to the Holy Lands, a violent storm began to rage and threaten the ship. Nicholas stretched his arms over the sea and prayed. At his words, the storm died away. St. Nicholas is the patron saint of children, sailors, fishermen, and murderers.

St. Lucy
December 13

St. Lucy was born into a very wealthy family. She was promised in marriage to a wealthy young man, but she refused him. He was so angry that he denounced her as a Christian to the governor. The governor then sentenced her to a horrible torture. When the guards came to take her away, they found that they could not move her. They even tried hitching her to a team of oxen, but she would not budge. She was then sentenced to death. She was tortured and had her eyes cut out. Finally, she was stabbed to death with a dagger. St. Lucy is the patron saint of eye disease, blind people, and writers.

Nativity of Our Lord
December 25

"And Joseph went up from Galilee, out of the city of Nazareth into Judea, to the city of David, which is called Bethlehem: because he was of the house and family of David, to be enrolled with Mary his espoused wife, who was with child. And it came to pass, that when they were there, her days were accomplished, that she should be delivered. And she brought forth her firstborn son, and wrapped him up in swaddling clothes, and laid him in a manger; because there was no room for them in the inn. And there were in the same country shepherds watching, and keeping the night watches over their flock. And behold an angel of the Lord stood by them, and the brightness of God shone round about them; and they feared with a great fear. And the angel said to them: Fear not; for, behold, I bring you good tidings of great joy, that shall be to all the people: For, this day, is born to you a Savior, who is Christ the Lord, in the city of David. And this shall be sign unto you. You shall find the infant wrapped in swaddling clothes, and laid in a manger. And suddenly there was with the angel a multitude of the heavenly army, praising God, and saying: Glory to God in the highest; and on earth peace to men of good will" (Luke 2:1-14).

St. Stephen
December 26

St. Stephen is the first martyr. He was chosen by the apostles to be one among the seven that were chosen to be the first deacons. He was a great preacher who spoke the truths of our faith in the streets. The Jews who were listening to him preach were infuriated by his message and believed him guilty of blasphemy. "When they heard these things they became enraged and ground their teeth at Stephen. But filled with the Holy Spirit, he gazed into heaven and saw the glory of God and Jesus standing at the right hand of God. 'Look,' he said, 'I see the heavens opened and the Son of Man tanding at the right hand of God!' But they covered their ears and with a loud shout, they dragged him out of the city and stoned him" (Acts of the Apostles, 7:54-58). With his dying breath, St. Stephen prayed for his persecutors. St. Stephen is the patron saint of deacons, coffin makers, and stone masons.

www.ingramcontent.com/pod-product-compliance
Lightning Source LLC
Chambersburg PA
CBHW081459040426
42446CB00016B/3319